Help!

My

cat's

too

fat

Help!
My
cat's
too
fat

Tony De Saulles

■SCHOLASTIC

For Janet

Thanks to the Cheltenham Animal Welfare Association
and also to Ollie the cat for his helpful contribution

Scholastic Children's Books,
Commonwealth House, 1-19 New Oxford Street,
London WC1A 1NU, UK

A division of Scholastic Ltd
London ~ New York ~ Toronto ~ Sydney ~ Auckland
Mexico City ~ New Delhi ~ Hong Kong

Published in the UK by Scholastic Ltd, 2002

Text and illustrations copyright © Tony De Saulles, 2002

ISBN 0 439 98281 2

All rights reserved

Printed by Cox & Wyman Ltd, Reading, Berks

2 4 6 8 10 9 7 5 3 1

The right of Tony De Saulles to be identified as author and illustrator of this work has been
asserted by him in accordance with the Copyright, Designs and Patents Act, 1988.

Contents

OUR FAMILY AND FRIENDS

Me, Beth.
(Aged ten)

My Dad, Doug
Kennel, The
Internet Vet

My brother,
Zak, with
Archie our cat

Mrs Pom-pom
Mr Fluffy
Uncle Ken
(Isle of Man)

Mau
Professor Kitty
Le Fez (Egypt)

Worldwide Web Award

"Ugh, I'm exhausted!" Dad sighed, collapsing into his chair.

"Excellent though, wasn't it?" I said, waving the strange object above my head.

Zak reached up and took the glass statue from me. "Careful!" he gasped. "We've worked hard for this. Don't go smashing it!"

We'd just got back from the Worldwide Web Awards (just in case you're wondering what I'm going on about). The WWW Awards are prizes presented to the best websites on the net. And as you've probably gathered – WE WON AN AWARD!

It was for Best New Animal Website and the competition was hot ... well, warm-ish. We were up against:

IS YOUR PUPPY REALLY SPOTTY?

AND YOUR BUDGIE ALWAYS SQUAWKING?

PODGY POODLES?
LAZY LIZARDS?
GET ON-LINE AND. . .

 Email your pet problems to me, Doug Kennel, The Internet Vet

 Post messages and photos on the Internet Pet Board

 Advertise your weird and wonderful pet products and remember:

IF YOUR PET'S UPSET CALL THE INTERNET VET!

Free pet advice – pretty good, eh? It all started when a new veterinary surgery opened down the road. It was totally trendy-looking and their charges were ridiculously cheap – just to attract new customers. OUR CUSTOMERS! Anyway, I had the brilliant idea of starting the website. So how does Dad make any money if the advice is free? Well, it's the Internet Vet Advertisements that bring in the dosh. People pay us to advertise their pet products. Dad writes the copy, I draw the pictures and Zak does all the boffiny bits ('cos that's what he is – a computer boffin). We have quite a laugh putting them together.

Zak put the WWW Award on top of the telly. "I bet that new surgery down the road hasn't got one of these," he said. "I reckon we should display it in our waiting room."

Dad yawned. "Absolutely, but now we all need some sleep. Who knows what pet problems we might be dealing with tomorrow."

I didn't know it at the time, but Dad was right. A new adventure involving blood-thirsty killings, revolting messes and incredible journeys was just around the corner. And it would start the next time I clicked the RECEIVE MAIL button…

CLICK!

Receive
Mail

Pyddle Hill

From: Daisy Braithwaite
Place: Pyddlehampton,
Yorkshire, England

Dear Internet Vet

Please help! – My life has been taken over by an enormous fat cat with no tail.

Since the stray turned up last week offering me half a mouse, he's been strutting around as if he owns the place. AND I DON'T EVEN LIKE CATS! At least I didn't think I did until this one turned up. But he's such a cool character. He purrs loudly on my lap while I feed him stuff.

And when I'm reading or drawing (my two favourite things!), he snoozes nearby. He even follows me on short walks! I don't know how he lost his tail but who cares? It kind of suits him!

Now I've told you the good bits, I'd better explain why I'm asking for help...

We've just moved from London to a house in the country. That's me (ten), Mum, Dad and the twins – Jemma and Josh (three and a half). Orchard Cottage is Mum and Dad's dream home – we're right on top of Pyddle Hill looking down on the town of Pyddlehampton.

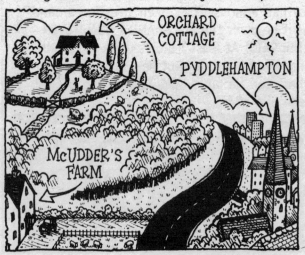

Dad promised it would be nice and quiet in the country, but it's not! Instead of car alarms and fire-engine sirens, I wake up to birds singing through  megaphones and horses clip-clopping backwards and forwards outside my bedroom window! Still, I'm sort of getting used to it and having Fat Cat around helps.

The twins saw him doing the "spraying thing" first. "Naughty Fat Cat!" they said crossly, pointing to him as he arched his back and squirted a disgusting-smelling spray against the kitchen-table leg.

And since then he's done it again twice. Yuk! Is he weeing? Why does he do it? And more importantly ... HOW CAN I STOP HIM?

Hope you can help,

Daisy Braithwaite

Dad raised his eyebrows. "That fat cat's almost as big as Gerty," He said. "He must be eating ten dinners a day!"

He'd just finished clipping Gerty the Great Dane's claws and he passed me the huge dog's lead.

"Daisy must think Fat Cat lost his tail in an accident," I said. "Will you explain what sort of cat he really is?"

"Maybe, but I'll deal with the spraying first. And I'm also worried that Fat Cat might belong to somebody else. Can you give Gerty back to her owners while I tap out an email, Betts?"

Hi Daisy

Spraying problems? I quite agree – the smell is disgusting! But it's a common problem, so don't panic!

You're right, Fat Cat is weeing. He's using his wee to scent-mark his territory. Spraying it on the furniture is a bit like putting up signs

This seems a little odd if he's never been to Orchard Cottage before. But something's stressing him, and I'm afraid it'll make matters worse if he's shouted at.

By the way, before you get too attached to this animal, I suggest that you take him to the nearest Animal Shelter. He might have a worried owner looking for him and if he's been microchipped the scanner will give you the owner's details.

However, if you do end up adopting Fat Cat, don't let him roam around the house. You'll need to make him a cosy little place of his own for a while – somewhere the twins won't bother him. He'll love it if you make him really comfy and you'll also need to feed him there, too. Cats don't tend to spray where they eat and sleep. (Well, would you!?) Once he's calmed down, the spraying should stop and Fat Cat can explore the rest of your house.

Take a look at the advert we've produced for the new No-Pong Spray. It's a brilliant invention and might be the answer to your prayers!

Lastly, Fat Cat looks ... TOO FAT! You'll need to watch his diet.

Good luck and let me know how you get on.

Doug Kennel, Internet Vet

PS Your fat friend hasn't lost his tail ... he's never had one. That's an interesting breed of cat you've got there!

INTERNET VET ADVERTISEMENTS

PURCHASE PET PRODUCTS FROM AROUND THE WORLD!

CAT SPRAYING PROBLEMS?

HOUSE SMELLS LIKE AN OLD TOILET?

FRIENDS STOPPED VISITING?

EVERYBODY GIVING YOU AIR FRESHENER FOR CHRISTMAS?

YOU NEED

NO-PONG SPRAY

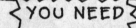

HOW DOES IT WORK?

Cats like to leave scent marks to let other cats know they're in town! They've got two ways of doing this.

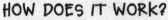

METHOD ONE: They spray their wee against things ... AND IT STINKS!

METHOD TWO: They rub their cheeks against objects. A gland in a cat's cheek emits a scent that humans can't smell. AND WHERE CATS USE CHEEK SCENT THEY DON'T USE THEIR WEE SCENT!

Wait a minute! you say

If somebody could make this cheek scent and put it into cans, we could spray it in the house and our cat wouldn't feel the need to squirt his wee everywhere!

We've already done it – it's called No-Pong!

NO-PONG SPRAY

HMMM! CHEEK SCENT. I WON'T BOTHER TO SPRAY MY WEE!

Your cat won't have THE CHEEK to spray again!

NO-PONG! STOPS A WEE PROBLEM BECOMING A BIG ONE!

The autumn half-term was over but I still found time to help Dad at weekends. The following Saturday we had a visit from Jim Bradshaw. He lives around the corner and called in with Barnacle, his old cat. The poor creature had been trapped under floorboards for several days and was very weak.

"Eeh, poor little beggar!" Jim said, lifting the bedraggled cat out of his box. "We 'ad builders in and Barney must 'ave crawled under the boards before they'd nailed them back down. Reckon 'e's been under there a fair while, Mr Kennel."

Dad agreed. "There's no broken bones, Jim. But old Barnacle's got quite a nasty graze on this back leg. We'd better keep an eye on him overnight and I'll give him an injection to fight off any infections he's picked up."

Jim shuffled off leaving Dad and me to sort Barnacle out.

The miserable-looking cat didn't put up much of a struggle as he received his injection. "There we go... good boy! I reckon he's only been under the floorboards for two or three days, Betts."

"Only two or three," I gasped. "He couldn't have survived much longer, could he?"

Dad raised his eyebrows. "Oh yes," he said. "I remember hearing about a cat that survived for 45 days in a similar situation. He must have been getting water from somewhere, but he hadn't eaten anything!"

"That's one and a half months!"

"Yeah, but he was OK." Dad chuckled. "Just a bit BOARD! Ha ha, get it? Floorboard, b-o-a-r-d, he was…"

"Yes, all right, Dad." I groaned. My dad's got a tragic sense of humour.

Then the office door opened.

"Email from Daisy Braithwaite!" Zak called out. Dad handed me the cat and disappeared into the office still calling out instructions. "Check that cat for fleas before you put him to bed!"

From: Daisy Braithwaite
Place: Yorkshire, England

Dear Internet Vet

Thanks for the advice.

We've just got back from the Animal Shelter. Fat Cat seemed pretty relaxed while they scanned him. He was enjoying the fuss and even decided to have a quick wash as the information appeared on the screen.

Guess what? His real name is *Rumpy* and he's a Manx cat. You're right, he *is* an interesting breed. And he didn't lose his tail in an accident 'cos Manx cats don't have tails – well most Manx cats, anyway.

That's how he got his name. Jan at the Animal Shelter said that a Manx cat with a tiny bit of tail is called a Stumpy and a Manx that has no tail at all is a Rumpy.

A DUMPY RUMPY

A GRUMPY STUMPY

We also found out Rumpy's home address. IT'S THE SAME AS OURS! Dad says Rumpy must

Rumpy Rake
Orchard Cottage
Pyddlehampton
Yorkshire

have belonged to the two sisters who lived in Orchard Cottage before us – Miss C Rake and Miss L Rake. He must have been stressed to find strangers in Orchard Cottage when he arrived back – that explains the spraying. Now we need to find where the sisters have moved to. Dad remembers them leaving their new address but he's lost it. Brilliant! And how on earth did Rumpy find his way back to Orchard Cottage?

I know we'll have to give him back eventually, but I'll enjoy looking after him until we contact the Rake sisters. He's such a loveable old thing, especially now he's stopped spraying! So even if it's only for a while, it's cool to be looking after such an unusual cat. I'm going to do some sketches of him this afternoon.

Oh, and can you tell me where Manx cats come from? Did they ever have tails? I'd love to read more about them. Can you help – please???

Best wishes
Daisy Braithwaite

PS There's a terrible racket going on outside. No, it's not Rumpy murdering another mouse – it's a huge tractor thing digging over the field next to our cottage.

I'd wandered into the office with Barnacle to look at the message.

"You know who's bound to have some info on Manx cats, don't you?" Dad said.

We answered together. "Uncle Ken!"

Uncle Ken is Dad's brother and he lives on the Isle of Man; the island where Manx cats first appeared.

I don't think he's actually got a Manx but he does have other pedigree cats and he enters them in cat shows all over the place. Uncle Ken's living room is full of shiny trophies. He also has hundreds of cat books. He'd be sure to have something for us.

In fact, we've got animal-mad relatives all over the world. Most of them are on email so we quite often send messages asking for help. It's a great way to get information and a brilliant way to keep in touch with everybody.

Zak went back to his work on the computer. "I'm just uploading this new Internet Vet Advert," he said. "I was going to make an animated GIF to show the little bloodsuckers leaping about, but the file was too large."

"What are you on about?" I said. "Just speak English, for goodness' sake!"

"I'm talking about cat fleas, durrrr! The advert is for an electric flea trap. It's pretty impressive, actually."

INTERNET VET ADVERTISEMENTS

PURCHASE PET PRODUCTS FROM AROUND THE WORLD!

THE CAT FLEA ZAPTRAP

Plug it in and sit back...

⚡ Watch as the fleas get trapped on the sticky pads!

⚡ Cheer as they're zapped by the electric current!

⚡ Jump for joy because the fleas won't ever jump again!

⚡ This could be the end of all your flea troubles!*

THIS IS SHOCKING!

I'M BEING ZAPPED!

ZAPTRAP SWITCH IT ON AND FLEAS CAN'T FLEE!

*SMALL PRINT. And then again, it might not. The traps might catch a few fleas but there will always be flea eggs waiting to hatch out in the carpet.

"Yeah, dead impressive till you read the small print," I scoffed. "Anyway, it's reminded me that we need to check Barnacle for fleas if he's staying in overnight. We don't want Archie or the other customers' cats catching them. Give us a hand, it's easier with two."

We took Barnacle back into the surgery. Zak tickled the cat's chin while I gave him a brush. The poor old thing seemed to quite enjoy it and appeared relaxed for the first time that day. Dad says that all cats should be brushed at least once a week. Especially old cats and fat cats 'cos they often can't reach all their body-bits!

It was time to check Barnacle for fleas! I held the brush over a sheet of dampened kitchen roll and ran my fingers through the bristles.

I checked the tissue closely for red spots. Why? Well, when a flea's been enjoying his favourite snack – fresh blood – he leaves tiny poos where he's been munching.

CHOMP!

POO!

We could be quite sure that Barnacle had fleas if little droppings of digested blood fell on to the damp tissue making red spots appear.

FLEAS!

NO FLEAS

"Phew! No flecks – he's fine," I said. "I'd better put the old mog to bed. He looks worn out."

Barnacle was soon curled up and snoozing away. After I'd emailed Uncle Ken I introduced myself to Daisy...

THE INTERNET VET

From: Beth (The Internet Vet's my dad)

Hi Daisy

I was interested to hear about Rumpy the Manx cat. My Uncle Ken knows quite a bit about them and I've just emailed him to ask for some info. I'll let you know when it comes.

Dad says cats who move house only a mile or so away often turn up at their old home. So maybe Rumpy's old owners live nearby? Weird isn't it?

Dad's showed me a magazine article about a German scientist who carried out a totally mad experiment to test cats' homing instincts. I've scanned it for you to have a look at.

THE A-MAZE-ING CAT EXPERIMENT

I AM TRYING TO FIND OUT HOW ZE CAT IS FINDING HIS WAY HOME FROM SOMEWHERE ZAT HE'S NEVER BEEN TO BEFORE!

CONTINUED ▶

The scientist puts a number of cats in boxes and drives them round the city.

Then he leaves the city and drives to a large field where he's made a huge maze.

Each cat is placed in the middle of the maze and left to choose from one of the 24 tunnels.

And did you see this amazing story in last week's paper?

KANSAS JOURNAL

SORE PAWS AND WORN-OUT CLAWS!

TOD HACK WITH ANOTHER TRUE-LIFE PET REPORT. THIS WEEK HE TELLS THE STORY OF A CAT THAT BECAME SEPARATED FROM ITS OWNER.

When Charlene Simpson went to work at Wisconsin Water Park last summer, she took her cat Skittles with her.

On 1 September, Charlene's job was finished and it was time to return home. But then disaster struck! Charlene discovered that Skittles had escaped from his travelling cage. She searched high and low but the cat had disappeared and a tearful Charlene had to return home without her furry friend. 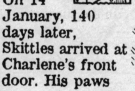 On 14 January, 140 days later, Skittles arrived at Charlene's front door. His paws

were sore and his ribs were showing as he wobbled into the house. Skinny Skittles had somehow managed to find his way home across 353 miles of open countryside.

Incredible, huh?

Hope to be in touch soon.

Best wishes

Beth Kennel

Daisy seemed to be enjoying looking after Fat Cat but I couldn't help wondering what had happened to the Rake sisters. The following Saturday, after helping in the surgery, I got an update…

Fish and Frogs

"Good boy! Shall I scratch your head? There we go. Shhhhhh, well done."

I'm quite good at calming nervous dogs for Dad when he needs to inject them.

"Keep it going, Betts, I'm nearly done."

"That's a good boy. That's it, you're all right, aren't you?"

The quivering dog gave a little yelp as the needle jabbed into the loose skin around his neck.

Dad looked pleased. "Well done!" he said, lifting Frankfurter the sausage dog on to the floor. "You won't be catching any deadly doggy diseases for a while, will you?"

I suppose the owner is usually the best person to calm a pet but Frankie's owner was 92 and not really up to the job. I walked the little hound back to his ancient owner in the waiting room.

"Thank you so much, my dear," Mrs Bratwurst croaked. "He's very precious to me, you know."

I knew what was coming next…

"I've had Dachshunds all my life, dear. Frankfurter's my eighth, you know and I'm 92."

"Yes, Mrs Bratwurst, that's right. Don't worry, he'll be safe for another year now."

"Eh? Oh yes, yes. Well, goodbye my dear."

And off she tottered. At last, I'd finished work for the morning and it was time to check the emails. Yippee, there was an update from Daisy!

From: Daisy Braithwaite

Hi Beth

Thanks for the email.

I suppose I knew we'd find Rumpy's owner sooner or later. And that's what's happened. I didn't think I'd be too bothered, but now he's back at his proper home, I really miss him! Actually, it wasn't Rumpy's real owner who took him away. I'll tell you what happened.

Yesterday was really sunny. I was sitting under the apple tree (drawing, as usual) with Rumpy chasing about like a nutcase after falling leaves.

A skinny, red-faced woman rattled up to us on her old bike. It was one of the Rake sisters and not only was she looking hot and bothered after cycling up Pyddle Hill – she was looking for Rumpy!

She seemed to cheer up a bit when she saw him. "Oh, thank goodness!" she sighed. "I've been looking high and low for this cat. He's been gone for well over two weeks. I never dreamt he'd get all the way back here! It's miles! What a naughty boy – and look – he's fatter than ever!"

I explained about losing her new address and not being able to bring her cat back.

"My cat? Oh good gracious, no!" she said. "Rumpy belongs to my sister, Camilla. I'm just looking after him while she's away on a world cruise. But he means the world to her. And I'm sure he must have used up one of his nine lives getting back to Orchard Cottage. He has to cross that main road!"

By this time, Rumpy was sitting on my lap and nudging me with his head. I'm sure he knew he was about to be taken away.

"And then there's the Furrington Cat Show in January. Camilla was keen to enter Rumpy. But how can she? He'll be the size of a pony by the time she gets home!"

Lizzy (that's her name) still seemed stressed even though she'd found what she was looking for. "Now then, Daisy, here's my email address. If Rumpy comes back, let me know and I'll cycle over. And please, please, don't feed him, dear. He's got to lose weight before Camilla returns."

She looked like the sort of person who'd be into fountain pens and letters rather than computers and emails. Still, I agreed to let her know if Rumpy came back.

Then, feeling a bit sad, I watched as Lizzy put Rumpy into a carrying cage, strapped it on to her bike and wobbled off down the hill.

So now I haven't got a cat of my own, I'll have to make do with reading about them. Weird, isn't it? I've never really wanted a cat but now I've looked after one ... well, never mind. Anyway, if you get that info on Manx cats, I'd still love to read it!

See you
Daisy

PS This afternoon I've got to help Mum and Dad pick some berries. They're going to squash them up and make wine, or something. They love all this "living in the countryside" stuff!

"I bet she's gutted that the owner turned up." Zak said when I told him about Daisy's email. "She needs one of those Kopy-Cat clones. Did you see that article? For the cost of about 30,000 tins of cat food, she could have an identical Rumpy all of her own!"

"What are you talking about?" I asked. "Is this one of your lame jokes?"

Zak didn't reply. Instead, he dashed upstairs and two minutes later plonked a magazine on the table. I could see from the headline that (for once) he wasn't joking at all…

KOPY-CAT CLONING— PAWS FOR THOUGHT?

Scientists in the USA claim to be able to make cat clones. Yes, that's right, **IDENTICAL COPIES OF YOUR OWN PET CAT!** IS THIS LEGAL? WHAT IS A CLONE? HOW DOES IT ALL WORK?

And is it possible to explain something so scientifically mind-boggling to somebody who looks like THIS rather than THIS?

We asked our expert to try…

CONTINUED ▶

DNA

EGG

Hairy Harry

Mumpuss

Scientists can take the DNA from one cat and inject it into the egg of another cat.

When Mumpuss gives birth to a kitten it will be an identical copy (a *clone*) of Hairy Harry!

But scientific opinions differ on the subject of cloning...

"For a start," says Doctor Cross of the MOANING-ABOUT-CLONING campaign, "Mumpuss's kitten might have identical genes to Hairy Harry but it could have slightly different markings!"

M.A.C

Professor Wright, head scientist at the Kopy-Cat Research Centre, defends his work. "But it's not just about looks," he explains. "Imagine the delight of recreating the character of a loved cat that has passed away. It will..."

"No, no, no!" interrupts Doctor Cross. "A cat's personality develops as it grows, it doesn't inherit it. And anyway, it's dangerous to play about with Mother Nature. You could create problems that you hadn't imagined!"

"Nonsense!" Professor Wright argues. "If scientists aren't allowed to experiment, as they have for hundreds of years, man will miss out on important discoveries."

Do you think people should be moaning about cloning or is Professor Wright ... right?

I chucked the magazine to Zak. "Well, if you ask me," I said, "it would be a total waste of money. Thirty thousand tins of cat food – that's about 10,000 quid! And all to produce a cat that could end up looking and acting differently from the pet it's supposed to be identical to."

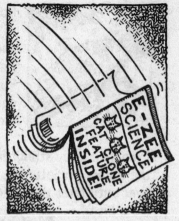

Zak turned to go. "Sorry for suggesting it," he said, and disappeared back to his room.

After school on Thursday I heard from Daisy again.

From: Daisy

Hi Beth

Thought I'd let you know the latest.

Rumpy had only been gone a few days when he was back again. He waddled across the lawn and dropped something dead at my feet. Then he rubbed his head against my legs and started purring! It was a present for me – that was quite clear.

How lovely. A dead fish with huge staring eyes and its guts hanging out! I'm sure it's very kind of Rumpy (not!) but why does he bring me these gruesome offerings?

I emailed Lizzy straightaway but she works in the library on Saturdays and couldn't cycle over until later that afternoon. Still, this won me a bit of time with my fat friend. I gave him a good brushing but he was looking even bigger than before, so I managed to resist feeding him.

Rumpy seemed so pleased to see me. That's what I love about him. He purrs softly when I stroke him and he always looks as if he's got a big smile on his face.

You should have seen Lizzy's face when she got up here. "Oh, Good Lord!" she wailed. "He's only been gone a couple of days and he's fatter than ever!"

Lizzy was horrified to hear about the fish and asked to see it. When I showed it to her, she went quite pale and said it was a valuable Koi carp, stolen from a neighbour's garden pond. Rumpy had done it before.

"That cat is quickly using up his nine lives!" she groaned. "Crossing busy roads and annoying our neighbours. Dear, oh dear!"

Before she cycled off, I suggested to Lizzy that she contact your dad about Rumpy's weight problem. Hope you don't mind. She doesn't want Camilla's vet to know about Rumpy getting so fat. Anyway, you might be getting an email quite soon. Camilla will be back in a month so I hope your dad can help!

Mail soon

Daisy

PS When we lived in the city there was a bus every ten minutes. There's only one bus a day up Pyddle Hill – that's why poor Lizzy has to cycle up here!

Still, it was downhill all the way back and I reckon Lizzy must have tapped out an email as soon as she got home.

From: Lizzy Rake
Place: Pyddlehampton,
       Yorkshire, England

Dear Internet Vet

I've just been given your details from young Daisy Braithwaite whom I believe you've been in contact with recently.

As I think you might know, I've been looking after my sister's cat and he's no longer the same size as he was when she left! He already has fairly small portions of tinned food but he eats so greedily that I'm reluctant to give him less. Daisy told me that she's already sent you a photo of him so you'll have some idea of my problem. Camilla will be returning from her world cruise in a few weeks. The truth is, Rumpy needs to lose weight – FAST!

Do you have any advice?

Thank you so much.

Yours truly

Lizzy Rake

Dad raised his eyebrows. "I seem to spend a lot of time giving advice to people with fat cats."

"Please help her," I said. "It sounds as if Camilla's going to be really cross. And don't forget she wants to enter Rumpy in the Furrington Cat Show."

Dad was looking thoughtful.

"And how come her sister gets to go on a world cruise while she stays at home and feeds the cat?" I continued.

"That's not really our business," Dad said. "But giving free pet advice is, so I'll drop her a line. And maybe you could do one of your special files? I've got loads of stuff on overweight cats. You could call it Useful Facts for Overweight Cats, or something. What d'you think?"

"Yeah, great!" I said. "But I think The Fat Cat File sounds better. Anyway, it would save you having to write loads of emails saying the same thing."

Dad was pleased. "You'd better check with Zak first, to see if he's got time."

I did – and he did. In fact he quite liked the idea. But we needed to work fast if The Fat Cat File was going to help Lizzy and Rumpy. In the meantime, Dad sent Lizzy a few pointers.

THE INTERNET VET

Hi Lizzy

You must be pleased to have Rumpy back home. And now that he is, you can help the fat cat to lose some weight.

Try feeding him three quarters of a normal portion of cat food (size of normal portion will be shown on box), AND NOTHING ELSE!

It's also possible that a neighbour might be feeding him. This could even be the main reason Rumpy's getting so fat. So ask around. If you can cut out any extra food he's getting, you'll have Rumpy slimmed down in no time!

I also suggest that you cut out the tinned food and try the dry stuff. It's cheaper, easier to feed, less smelly and just as good for them.

It's also better for their teeth! In the wild, a cat's teeth would be kept clean by the crunching of bones! Dry cat food helps to keep teeth clean in much the same way.

One last thing. Ever tried eating two cream crackers without a drink? Well, that's how Rumpy will feel if he doesn't have a big bowl of water by his dry food!

Good luck
Doug Kennel

PS My children, Beth and Zak, are compiling one of their web files at the moment. I think they're planning to call it The Fat Cat File. It'll be packed full of info so we'll let you know as soon as it's up and running on the site.

A few days later we heard from the Isle of Man. Not an email but a letter. Good old Uncle Ken, I knew he'd come up with something.

Dear Doug, Zak and Beth

How are you all? I was very interested to hear about Daisy and her Manx cat. How exciting! And I noticed that she lives quite near Furrington – perhaps I'll bump into her when I visit the Furrington Cat Show in January!

Mr Fluffy, my champion Persian, won "Best In Show" last year – what a beautiful glass vase we received! I was so thrilled I treated both Mr Fluffy and Mrs Pom-pom to a new sequin collar. Beautiful!

Anyway, while I was looking through my cat files I discovered something interesting. As you know, I teach at the local junior school. Last term they had to write about their pets. One lad called his project THE TALE OF THE MANX CAT. His parents actually breed Manx cats so he knows quite a bit about them. Anyway, I thought his project was quite funny and I thought you (and Daisy) might like to see it...

THE TALE OF THE MANX CAT

by Warren Wilkins (aged eight)

HOW DID MANX CATS LOSE THEIR TAILS?

The first Manx cats came from our little island what is called the Isle of Man and it is in the sea near England. There are lots and lots of Manx cats living on our island but lots of others have been taken away to live with peeple in their houses around the world.

Why do peeple fall in love with Manx cats all the time? It is because they are clever and friendly and good at caching mice. The only thing they are not good at is having a tail. My mum and dad have told me stories about what happened to Manx cats' tails.

One story says that the Manx cat had his tail chopped off when Noah shut it in the door of the ark!

Another story rekons that Noah's dog, bited the cat's tail off.

A man called Joseph Train, who is dead now, wrote in his diary that

Rabbit cat

because Manx cats hop about like what rabbits do and because they don't have tails, they must be half cat and half rabbit. He called them cabbits.

But that was in the old days and scientists say that the man was wrong. They say that the missing tail thing is something (Dad calls it a deformity) that is passed from a mother cat to her kittens.

mother cat

kittens

Sometimes the deformity can be really, really, really bad. So bad that kittens are born with wonky back legs. That is why sometimes they hop about like rabbits do.

hop!

hop!

HOW DID THE MANX CAT GET TO THE ISLE OF MAN?

Some pe**o**ple say that there were cats without tails onb**o**rd Spanish ships 400 years ago. The Spanish pe**o**ple had got the cats from Japan when they went there. There was a big fight between the Spanish ships and the English ships. Pe**o**ple say that cats without tails swum to the be**a**ch from a ship that had crashed into a rock.

I'm drownin', me harties!

meow!

curses!

meow!

glug!

Other peeples reckon that hundreds of years ago, men from Japan had cats without tails. The cats jumped on to land when the Japanese ships were visiting the Isle of Man. Or the first Manx cat could have been a sailor's pet that had been brought back from the other side of the world. ··✳

You are looking jolly, Roger. What is that you have got there?

MANX CATS TODAY

These days there are both short and long-haired types of Manx cat. And you can have different colours like black, white, tabby, tortoiseshell and all sorts! If you see a cat without a tail and want to know if it is a Manx or just a cat what's had an accident, this pixture will help you.

bum in the air
round face
no tail
back legs longer than front legs
big round eyes

OK, so his spelling's not great, but he's got his facts right and it did make me chuckle!

Love to everybody
Uncle Ken
(+ Mr Fluffy and Mrs Pom-pom)

Zak and I were both reading the letter when Dad came in.

"Uncle Ken's sent us some Manx stuff," I said. "The spelling's a bit dodgy but it's quite a laugh. It's something one of his pupils did."

"Trust Ken," Dad chuckled. "Don't forget to send it all to Daisy."

So that's what I did before getting on with my homework. Of course, Zak had already finished his. The creep! So he decided to start work on The Fat Cat File.

A couple of days later I was working on The Fat Cat File too, with Archie snoozing next to me. I heard Dad calling upstairs.

"Hey Betts, there's an email for you!"

From: Daisy

Hi Beth

Guess what? Rumpy's back!

We were watching telly earlier when there was a knock at the door. Mum opened it but there was nobody there. Two minutes later there was another knock so I opened it this time. And there was Rumpy – with a frog in his mouth! He must have been lifting the door knocker with his paw to get our attention. He's so clever (though I don't suppose the frog thought so).

The twins didn't appreciate having their telly-viewing interrupted. "Stop making noise, naughty fat cat!" they wailed. So after disposing of the dead frog (I'm getting good at dealing with mangled bodies), I took Rumpy into the dining room and gave him a brush. First I emailed Lizzy. Then, with Rumpy by my side, I put a message on the Internet Pet Board. You may have seen it.

Thanks for the Manx cat stuff – I thought the drawings were really sweet! The bit about Manx cats being clever and friendly is certainly true – look at Rumpy. Maybe that's how cats became pets in the first place – they charmed their way into homes with offerings of dead frogs. Seriously though, how did it happen? Who were the first people to keep cats?

Bye for now
Daisy

PS Lizzy said she'd forgotten all about Rumpy's door knocker trick! Her new house only has an electric bell!

Hmm, I'd never really thought about who'd kept the first pet cats. I'd have to ask Dad.

Zak was tapping something into the computer. "Daisy didn't say what her message on the Pet Board was about," Zak said. "Let's take a look!"

THE INTERNET PET BOARD

TALK TO PET OWNERS AROUND THE WORLD!

Post your message on The Internet Pet Board:
Questions – jokes – photos –
fascinating facts – in fact, anything that
other pet lovers will find interesting.

Message from:
Daisy Braithwaite
(aged ten), England
Hello everybody. I've recently met an amazing Manx cat called Rumpy. I don't know why, but he brings me a different present every time he visits. First it was a mouse, then a fish, and tonight ... a frog! He even uses the door knocker when he wants to be let in. Are there any other clever cats out there?

Tabetha Pussoski, Hungary

Hello Daisy

I thought Smoggy, my beautiful grey cat, was the only puss who brought strange things home. She might not be the cleverest cat in the world but she's probably the naughtiest! In the summer she steals children's toys from gardens. Last year she brought me two teddy bears, a purple koala, a rubber giraffe and a musical tortoise!

Nick Dinnerz, USA

Hi Guys

I've gotta cat burglar, too. Tealeaf's not too bothered about furry animals, though. He's more into other folks' suppers. Sniffing out something real tasty, he strolls right in through open windows and steals whatever he fancies. So far he's stolen: a frozen chicken, some kippers, half a pound of sausages and a large piece of steak.

Rob Naybers, Germany

I too have a naughty cat. His name is Claus and he is the cause of much embarrassment! He likes to steal underwear from other people's houses. He has presented me with 11 different socks, three pairs of knickers and four pairs of pants.

 Perhaps you are saying this is not embarrassing? But it's not you who has to call on your neighbours to ask if they are missing a pair of pants! Now I think you are understanding the situation. Yes?

Walter Wall, Sweden

Don't be cross with your cats, guys! They are bringing you gifts because you are part of their family. And unless you want to be keeping them locked indoors all day there's no way you'll stop them catching stuff! Your cats think you are useless at hunting (maybe they're right!) and are trying to show you how it's done. So the next time Smoggy, Tealeaf or Claus bring you a mouse or a pair of pants, don't scream, say "Thanks!"

Zak was impressed. "They make our cat sound really boring," he said. "Some days, Archie even forgets how to use his cat flap!"

Saturday soon arrived. By lunchtime we'd treated: a spaniel with an ear infection, a chipmunk with teeth problems, a parrot who was losing his feathers and, lastly, Barnacle the cat. The graze was healing quickly and there was no sign of infection. Poor old Barnacle still had a bald bum where Dad had shaved his fur (to clean the graze) but other than that he was fine.

Over lunch and with a mouthful of baked beans, I asked Dad who'd first had the bright idea of keeping cats as pets.

"Er, well, I think it's possible that the, er, maybe the…" he said.

"You don't know, do you?" I laughed.

"Well no, I'm not an expert on cat history," he admitted. "But … I know somebody who is. I've got a very old friend in Egypt called Kitty Le Fez. She's been studying cats for years."

Dad was smiling now – pleased to have got himself off the hook.

"Great, I'll contact her! What's the email address?"

Now he was grinning.

"Don't worry, Betts. I'll do it."

To: Professor Kitty Le Fez
c/o Museum of the Ancient Cat, Cairo, Egypt

Dearest Kitty

How are you? It seems a long time ago that we were driving through the desert in that old Landrover. Good times, eh? And do you remember that incident with the angry camel? Could have been nasty!

(found this old photo!!)

Have you finished your studies yet? I was
hoping that you might be able to email me
some info on cats. One of my clients (a young
girl called Daisy) has been asking who first
kept cats as pets. Do you have anything on
this? (Not in hieroglyphics, please!) Hope to
hear from you soon.

Love
Dougy xx

Dad nipped back to the surgery but I stayed to read
his email. Who was this Kitty Le Fez? I didn't
remember Dad ever telling me about a trip through a
desert in an old Landrover. I was just about to go and
quiz him on the matter when an email came through
from Daisy. I printed a copy to take up to Zak – Kitty
Le Fez would have to wait.

"Back in a minute, Dad," I called out. "Things are
getting interesting!"

Collar the Culprit

Zak looked up from the computer screen. "The Fat Cat File's nearly ready."

"Never mind that!" I said. "Take a look at this."

From: Daisy Braithwaite

HELP!

Hi Beth

As soon as Lizzy gets Rumpy home, he turns around and comes straight back up here! Today, he brought me a dead rabbit. The twins were horrified. "Naughty fat cat. Poor bunny!" they said. And it was a big bunny, too! Honestly, Dad's vegetable patch is starting to look like an animal graveyard! As I bent down to pat Rumpy's head and thank him for the delicious prezzie, I noticed something ...

HE WAS WEARING A RED COLLAR!

Who gave it to him? It certainly wasn't me and I know it wasn't Lizzy. She said your Dad thought a neighbour might be feeding him and we reckon this proves it. No wonder he's so fat! And not only are they feeding him – if they've bought him a collar they must think they own him! Who are they? It could be anybody in Pyddlehampton. What should we do?

Daisy

PS When Lizzy emailed me back she said she'd pick Rumpy up in the morning. I didn't feed him but I let him sleep on my bed! I think the walk up Pyddle Hill must have tired him out 'cos he didn't move all night!

Zak read the message. "Interesting!" he said, and went back to clicking away with his mouse. "I've uploaded my HTML files onto the ISP and I had a bit of trouble with the CGI bin 'cos the pearlscript went wonky! But it's sorted now."

"Well done," I replied. I didn't have the faintest clue what he was jabbering on about.

Dad was examining a rabbit. He was peering up its nose when … IT SNEEZED!

"UGH!" he gasped. Yellow snot dribbled down Dad's cheek. We tried not to laugh as he plonked the rabbit back in its basket and took off his glasses to clean them.

Dad held them up to the light and checked for snot splatters. He seemed to think we were waiting for an explanation.

"She's got snuffles; like a sort of bad cold," Dad said. "I'll need to make sure that her hutch is well ventilated and that she's not being stressed by any other animals. A course of antibiotics will also be necessary, just in case there's any secondary infection."

"That's really fascinating, Dad," I said, handing him the email. "But we just wanted to show you this."

Dad studied the print-out, nodding his head wisely. "I thought as much," he said. "I suggest that they send a message to the mystery feeder."

He was missing the point. "But they don't know who it is or where they live."

"No problem," he replied. "They can attach a message to Rumpy's new collar."

Brilliant. Why didn't we think of that?

Dad checked The Fat Cat File. He corrected a few spelling mistakes, had a laugh, and gave us the go-ahead. I think he liked it.

"Time to contact Daisy," I said. "Or should I be emailing Lizzy?"

"Just copy the same email to both of them, durrr!" Zak said, practical as ever. "And hurry up, 'cos I want to get The Fat Cat File up and running!"

THE INTERNET VET

From: Beth
To: Daisy
Cc: Lizzy

Hi, you two!

Fascinated to hear about the collar. Dad suggests you attach a message to it. Tell whoever it is to STOP FEEDING RUMPY!

Also, The Fat Cat File will be up and running any minute now. There are loads of useful tips to help with Rumpy's weight problem.

Hope you manage to slim him down before Camilla gets back.

Good luck
Beth

I clicked "send" then Zak took over to do his stuff. It wasn't long before we were admiring our handiwork.

THE INTERNET VET

FAT CAT FILE

Hi! I'm Dr Ali Katari, world famous cat health expert.

Only yesterday, one of the tubbiest tabbies I've ever seen was dragged into my surgery by his desperate owner. Boy, was he big! His name was Blobzilla...

THE EXAMINATION

GRRR!

Your owner's worried you won't live long if you don't fight the flab NOW! You certainly look large. But let's do some proper checks.

69

THE DIAGNOSIS

Your owner is right, you ARE too fat! So how are we going to slim you down?

ERK!

We could try scaredy-cat tactics? Take a look at this sad case. Himmy was a male tabby who lived in Australia. He's the heaviest cat ever recorded and died young in 1986 weighing 21.3 kg (47 lb) Which is about the same weight as five average cats put together!

OOF!

Now, before I can treat you, I need to know how you got so fat. If you've put on weight without eating more than you should, you might already be ill.

HUH?

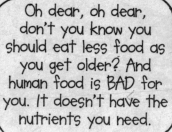 

Oh dear, oh dear, don't you know you should eat less food as you get older? And human food is BAD for you. It doesn't have the nutrients you need.

DOH!

THE TREATMENT

First of all, I'm advising your owner to lock up the cat flap! It's for your own good. You're putting a strain on your internal organs. Fat cats can suffer from horrible diseases, you know!

GASP!

Next – a plan I've developed to help fat cats get slim. It's called the FC Plan...

1. Eat less! Three quarters of a normal portion will help you to lose weight and stay healthy.

2. STOP eating human scraps and refuse any treats.

3. NO milk for you - water is much better!

4. Take MORE exercise. Start following your owners around the house. Just a few trips up and down the stairs for ten minutes each day will work wonders!

10 mins

5. KEEP PLAYING! That's the good news - playing keeps you fit not fat! Your owner will need to get you some cat toys. I'll give them one of these leaflets.

ATTENTION CAT OWNERS!

Fishing-rod toys are easy to make and a good way to give your fat cat some extra exercise! Most cats like catnip toys (catnip is a plant that seems to get cats excited!) so tie one of these on your rod and give your cat a good work-out!

TOY MOUSE STUFFED WITH CATNIP

"Your friend Lizzy will have to get cracking if she wants Rumpy slim before her sister gets back. She's only got three weeks," Zak said.

"She needs to find the mystery feeder first. What's the point of diets and exercises if somebody down the road is stuffing Rumpy with food?"

Zak nodded. "Maybe she'll need to lock his cat flap, and keep him away from whoever's feeding him."

"Not if Dad's message idea works," I said. "I wonder if they've sent it yet."

A couple of days later we found out…

Nobby No-tail

From: Daisy

HELP!

Hi Beth

Well it worked. In fact, it worked a little too well!

First of all, Lizzy says thanks for thinking of it and thanks also for The Fat Cat File. It really cheered her up and she thinks it'll be very useful. She's a bit busy trying to sort everything out at the moment (as you'll understand when I've explained), so I'm writing to put you in the picture.

Lizzy wrote a message and attached it to the red collar.

METAL CAPSULE
MESSAGE

To: Whoever's feeding this cat
From: MissLizzy@Rake.co.uk

I'm looking after my sister's cat, Rumpy, while she's away. It was very kind of you to buy him a collar but he's not a stray. And please don't feed him - he's becoming far too fat!

I'd be grateful if you'd send an email to let me know that you've received this message. And please pop it back in the tube in case anybody else needs to read it!

It wasn't long before an email came through (she forwarded everything to me):

To: Miss Lizzy Rake
From: Matt Pawsworth (age nine)

Sorry, Miss Rake, we wondered where Nobby No-tail came from. He calls on us every few days and I usually give him a piece of choccy, which he loves.

Mum says to tell you that we didn't buy the collar and that we won't feed him any more. I hope he still visits, though.

So was it the choccy that was making Rumpy so fat? Well ... no, because Matt wasn't the only person feeding him:

To: *Madam Rake*
From: *Pierre Pallette (sculptor and fine artist)*

Ooh-la-la, Mr Big has an owner! I must confess I had my suspicions. How could he be expanding so fast? I mean, yes, he does like to share the occasional curry with me. But only once or twice a week! It has been nice to have

a fat cat snoozing in the window of my studio but I will stop feeding him immediately.

You have my word.

Pierre

PS That collar's nothing to do with me!

Chocolate, curries ... and that wasn't all:

To: *Miss Elizabeth Rake*
From: *Father Sean McHat*

Dear Miss Rake

The Lord works in mysterious ways. I must confess that I've been worrying about this

77

tail-less cat wandering round my church at odd times of the night and day.

I'd named Fat Franky after Saint Francis, the patron saint of animals, and now my prayers to him have been answered. Sure, I haven't minded giving the big fella some of my sardines on toast, but now I know he has a loving owner, rest assured, I'll not be sharing my meals with him any longer.

God bless you for putting me in the picture.

Father Sean

PS Heaven knows who put the collar on him – I didn't!

A small boy, an artist and a priest – what next?

To: Miss Rake
From: WPC Dixon, Pyddlehampton police station

Hello Miss Rake

I'm afraid my colleagues and I have been guilty of feeding the cat with no tail we call Plod (but we're not guilty on the Collar charge). We thought he was just a stray when he plodded into the station and we've been feeding him crisps from the vending machine. He doesn't stay long, mind, just scoffs a bag of prawn cocktail and wanders off (usually in the direction of the Daily Pyddle offices). We hope you'll let us off with a caution this time. We promise not to feed him any more.

Regards
WPC Dixon

And down the road from the police station are the offices of the Daily Pyddle...

To: Lizzy Rake
From: Terry Ball (Editor of the Daily Pyddle)

HOLD THE FRONT PAGE! So Ed has an owner? But we love him! He first wandered into our office (think he came in through the loo window) a few weeks ago. He loves a saucer of cold tea and a tuna sandwich. What a character! Still, I appreciate that you need to slim him down a bit. So relax, we'll stop feeding him!

Terry Ball

By the way – I don't know anything about the collar.

And the last one was from the farm at the bottom of the hill:

To: Lizzy Rake
From: Freda McUdder

Apologies Lizzy, I'm afraid we thought old Doublecream was a stray. We get quite a few cats that hang around the farm feeding off the mice in the barns. (But we wouldn't bother to

put a collar on any of them!) These mousers do a good job for us and Doublecream's one of the best. That's

*how he got his name – we used to reward him
with a saucer of cream, fresh from the milking
parlour. But we
understand your problem
and Doublecream will get
no more double cream
from us!*

*Best wishes
Freda*

Amazing, huh? And everybody had a different
name for him. What's more, looking on the
map I've realized something else. If you draw
a line from each place he visits to the next,
including Orchard Cottage, it shows Rumpy's
route from Lizzy's house to ours! It seems that
he's been calling in at these places on his way
up to the top of Pyddle Hill.

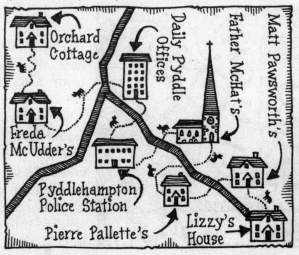

81

So he really wants to live here with me. I wish he could, he's the best cat ever. Poor old Rumpy!

Lizzy's emailed all the feeders to thank them for contacting her. There must be at least one more feeder out there, though, 'cos we still don't know who bought the collar!

Love from
Daisy

What a story! And if she could find "Collar Person", Lizzy would have stopped all Rumpy's extra meals. Surely then he'd start losing some weight!

Zak was as gobsmacked as me. "That fat cat sure has a lot of friends."

"Yeah," I agreed. "But he likes Daisy best. That's why he keeps going back."

A few days later we heard from Kitty Le Fez. Dad went a bit pink when I told him his "friend" had emailed us.

After having a good read, I sent the info on to Daisy.

To: Dougy
From: Kitty Le Fez
Place: Museum of the Ancient Cat,
Cairo, Egypt

Great to hear from you, Dougy.

Kalik and Mustapha say, "Hi!" They laughed when I reminded them about the angry camel incident! We enjoyed some special times.

Anyway, to answer your question – yes, I'm still into cats in a big way! Part of my work in the Museum has been to create some huge cartoon-strip panels. They are brightly lit and children love to read them as they wander around the exhibits. It's a great way to teach history! We've put them on our website, too. I've attached the files.

Last year I rescued a skinny cat from the streets of Cairo. I've named him Mau (the Ancient Egyptian word for cat) and I've made him the main character in the cartoon strips! Cats like Mau are not honoured as they were thousands of years ago in Ancient Egypt...

Hi guys! My name's Mau and I come from the streets of Cairo. Before the Prof took me back to her pad, I used to spend my days scratching about looking for food: mouldy bread, maggoty meat, even rotten fish. Man, when you're starving you'll eat anything!

But it wasn't like this when we first got together with humans. No way! They needed us back then. How long ago? It's kind of hard to say – maybe five or six thousand years...

MAKING FRIENDS!

THIS NEW FARMING LARK IS HARD WORK!

YEAH, IT'S TAKEN ALL SUMMER TO GROW THAT CORN.

MUNCH!

NIBBLE!

SCOFF!

CHEW!

AND NOW THOSE MICE ARE SCOFFING IT!

MAYBE THEY'LL STAY FOR GOOD.

WE CAN'T CALL THEM THAT!

TOO LONG. "CATCHERS" MAYBE?

HERE, FURRY-THING-WITH-WHISKERS!

HOW ABOUT "MICE-CATCHERS"?

"CATS" SOUNDS BETTER.

No fooling, that's how people and cats got friendly — well maybe not the bit about how cats got their name!

MICE ONE!

PURRRRRFECT!

Nobody's sure who were the first dudes to invite cats into their homes. But we know those Ancient Egyptian guys kept them 3,500 years ago because...

SACRED PETS

They drew pictures of their pets!

LICK!

I WISH HE'D KEEP STILL!

They made statues of them, too.

CRUNCH!

LOOK AT ME-OW!

They even made jewellery for their cats.

IT'S OK TILL YOU GET IT CAUGHT ON A BRANCH!

In fact ... they worshipped them! Every spring in Ancient Egypt, half a million people gathered for the Festival of the Cat where they honoured the cat-goddess Bastet.

PRAY! PRAISE! WORSHIP! EXALT!

Man, I should have been around then. We had respect!

All cats were considered sacred. The punishment for killing one was ... DEATH!

IT WASN'T ME!

Even if a cat died of old age or natural causes the whole family went into mourning and shaved off their eyebrows as a mark of respect!

I'M GONNA MISS HIM!

SHAVE! SHAVE!

YEAH, SOB, BLUB!

Dead cats were mummified – their bodies were soaked in chemicals and wrapped in bandages. Sometimes, the mummies were put in little cat-shaped coffins. Then they were buried with other cat mummies – millions of them!

These days, the breed that is thought to look most like the cats of the Ancient Egyptians is the Spotted Egyptian Mau.

That's me, man!   And that's my mummy!

EGYPTIAN MAU

I hope Daisy finds this interesting.

By the way, congratulations on your WWW Award. Kalik, Mustapha and I took a look at your Internet Vet site last night. It's fab!

Love and best wishes
Kitty xxx

I passed the info on to Daisy. And this reply came two days later:

From: Daisy

Hi Beth

Thanks for the Mau story – I really enjoyed reading it.

I've just had an email from Lizzy. She's really frustrated with not being able to find "Collar Person". All the other feeders have agreed to stop but somebody out there still thinks Rumpy belongs to them.

Even worse, Lizzy plans to keep Rumpy indoors until Camilla comes home! It's not just because of "Collar Person" – Lizzy says that every time Rumpy walks up Pyddle Hill to Orchard Cottage he uses one of his  nine lives to cross the main road. She says that taping up his cat flap will sort both problems in one go. But I'm not so sure – I've learned loads about cats in the last few weeks and it seems to me that they're pretty good at looking after themselves.

Poor Rumpy! The taped-up cat flap means he'll be on his own all day and not able to visit me. Lizzy says I can call in at weekends. Now she's stopped all Rumpy's extra meals she says she needs to concentrate on getting him slim.

The only good news is that I've been looking for an idea for my school project. It has to be about animals and all this talk about cats having nine lives has got me thinking. When I've finished it I'll show Lizzy. It might help Rumpy!

Love
Daisy

PS Hope you don't mind but I've put another message on the Pet Board!

Hmm, so what was this school project? How on earth could it help Rumpy? And why was Daisy putting messages on the Pet Board? Maybe it was just a way to cheer herself up. Even so, I considered it my duty (being an extremely nosy person) to see what she was up to.

THE INTERNET PET BOARD

TALK TO PET OWNERS AROUND THE WORLD!

Post your message on The Internet Pet Board:
Questions – jokes – photos –
fascinating facts – in fact, anything that
other pet lovers will find interesting.

Message from: Daisy Braithwaite (age ten), England

Hello everybody
I've got another cat question!
Have cats really got nine lives?

Lars Stinline, Finland

Hello Daisy
Of course cats don't have nine lives ... but it might seem that they do! Cats often survive life-threatening situations using their brilliant eyesight, balance, hearing, smell and taste. Perhaps this is how the "nine lives" superstition came about. Take a look at my super-cat, Lenny:

NINE-LIVES LENNY

SUPERSENSITIVE WHISKERS

EXCELLENT HEARING

SUPER-SMELL DETECTOR

INCREDIBLE EYESIGHT

POWERFUL LEG MUSCLES

Living with humans has also helped keep cats safe through the ages. A thousand years ago, good mousers were highly valued and well looked after!

Pete's Petshop, England
Wotcha Daisy
Yeah, old Lars is spot on! My old man used to run this gaff before me and I remember something the old boy had pinned up at the back of the shop. I've still got it now. It's a copy of an old poster talking about the price of cats a thousand years ago. They were worth a fortune – a blimin' site more than the hamsters and goldfish I sell, anyway! I've attached a copy:

The Cost of Ye Mouser-Cat

 A kitten, before it be able to see = one penny

 A kitten that can see but before it be catching a mouse = two pence

 A cat that be a great catcher of mice = four pence

Further more, it is decreed in law that anybody stealing or killing one of the King's cats who be guarding the Royal Granary, will be fined as much wheat as it takes to cover a dead cat that be hanging from its tail with its head touching the floor.

Four pence might not sound much to pay for a cat but 1,000 years ago that would have been about £400. Blimey, you could buy 100 gerbils for that!

Jocasta Spell, Germany

Good day to you, Daisy.

It is fascinating to read Peter's poster from 1,000 years ago. Five hundred years later, things were very different for cats. Having even nine lives wasn't much help!

Because cats had been worshipped in the old religions that had gone before Christianity, they were punished in terrible ways. Such cruelty! Christians really believed that cats were evil! The poor animals were beaten, roasted and even thrown from the top of church towers. And many old women who owned cats were accused of being witches and burnt at the stake with their pets.

Yes, the Middle Ages were dark, suspicious times ... especially for cats!

Dr Pierre Curie, France

Suspicious times? Ah yes, indeed. And at other times in history, cats have had to give up all nine of their lives in order to save one human life. Especially in medicine. Pete's poster reminded me of an illustration I have in one of my medical books. I doubt if the remedies below would have helped the patient and they certainly wouldn't have done the cat much good!

YE OLDE CAT CURES

The mysterious and magical qualities of the cat have been said to cure all sorts of human illnesses. So if you've got one of the following problems and you also own a cat (ideally black) ... YOU'RE IN LUCK!

SPOTS? – Try the old Roman remedy: cat poo mixed with a little mustard and rubbed on the affected area. (Hope you haven't got spots in your mouth!)

BLINDNESS? – Blind and living in the Middle Ages? Don't panic, just burn the head of a black cat to powder and rub it on your eyes!

THAT'S YOUR NOSE!

WARTS? – Give the ancient Canadian cure a go. Rub butter on your warts and get your cat to lick it off.

YUK!

BURNS? – Just been burnt in the Great Fire of London? No probs – skin a dead cat, then put the fur against your burnt bits for immediate relief.

SIZZLE!

Yuk! I wouldn't want to have been a cat back then, even if I had 90 lives!

So I'd checked out the Pet Board but I still wasn't sure what Daisy was up to.

Rumpy's Prison

We were sitting in our warm, brightly-lit office looking out on a cold wet day.

"Wonder how Rumpy's getting on in his prison," Zak said.

"Don't suppose he'd fancy being out in this," I answered. "But I'll bet he's bored – he loves being out and about."

Dad was listening in. "Lizzy needs to keep that fat cat entertained."

"Yeah, like cats are really into Playstations!" Zak laughed. I told him to button it. Dad obviously had something in mind.

"It'll be two weeks before Camilla gets back," I said. "What do you suggest?"

Dad took the computer mouse and started clicking. "Remember those adverts we did for Pet Tapes? I reckon they might keep Rumpy amused while Lizzy's at work. She could set them to come on through the day." He was scrolling down a menu list. "Ah, here we are!"

INTERNET VET ADVERTISEMENTS

PURCHASE PET PRODUCTS FROM AROUND THE WORLD!

OUT AT WORK ALL DAY? CAT SHUT INDOORS? WORRIED THAT HE'S BORED? WELL NOW HE CAN STAY IN AND HAVE A GOOD TIME WITH...

MOGGY-GOGGLE-BOX TAPES

Sit him within clawing distance of the screen* and he'll have hours of fun.

TAPE 1. BUGS GALORE! Your cat will get a real buzz watching all these crawling, hopping and flying insects.

TAPE 2. BIRD BONANZA! Time will fly by when your cat's watching this tape. Hours of flapping, squawking, pecking and nest building. Eggs-ellent value!

*Make sure you remove all glass vases and china ornaments from the top of the TV. We can't be held responsible for any breakages!

Zak was impressed. "Nice idea, Dad! I'd forgotten about those."

I emailed Dad's suggestion to Lizzy, then helped feed the pets that were staying with us overnight.

The following day we heard from Daisy. The email had a file attached – was this what I thought it was?

From: Daisy
To: Beth
Cc: Lizzy

Hi Beth and Lizzy

Thought you might like to see my school project. I showed it to the twins but they walked off before I'd finished the first page! Maybe they're too young. Anyway, I've attached a file. Let me know what you think.

ANIMAL STUDY PROJECT by Daisy Braithwaite, year 6, Pyddlehampton Junior School.

THE SUPERSENSIBLE CAT

(or, WHY RUMPY'S STILL GOT NINE LIVES)

It's a freezing autumn night as Rumpy pushes through his cat flap and looks up at the full moon shining over Pyddle Hill.

MAN, I'M GLAD TO BE OUT OF THERE!

Suddenly, Rumpy sees a car reversing up the drive towards him. Using his whiskers to judge the gap, Rumpy squeezes through a tight hole in Lizzy's garden fence and escapes.

SURVIVAL SKILL 1

USING THEIR WHISKERS AND SENSITIVE BODY HAIRS TO JUDGE GAPS ACCURATELY, CATS QUICKLY DISCOVER ESCAPE ROUTES.

NO PROBS!

He stares up at a high wall, lit in the pale moonlight. On the other side is a 15-metre drop. Using his super-sensitive eyesight he leaps to the top, judging the distance perfectly.

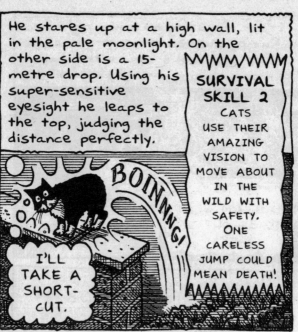

SURVIVAL SKILL 2 CATS USE THEIR AMAZING VISION TO MOVE ABOUT IN THE WILD WITH SAFETY. ONE CARELESS JUMP COULD MEAN DEATH!

BOINNNG!

I'LL TAKE A SHORT-CUT.

Rumpy hears a strange noise and dives for cover. Milliseconds later, a gritting lorry appears from round the corner and zooms past, showering the icy roads with salt.

SURVIVAL SKILL 3 HAVING EXCELLENT HEARING HELPS CATS TO AVOID LIFE-THREATENING SITUATIONS.

THAT WAS CLOSE!

BLAST!

Rumpy finds himself outside Pyddlehampton Police Station. This time his large ears recognize the voices of friends. He strolls inside to see them.

EH UP, PLOD! WHAT YOU AFTER, THEN?

CRISPS!

SURVIVAL SKILL 4 - BEING ABLE TO CHARM HUMANS IS ANOTHER SURVIVAL SKILL THAT'S HELPED CATS SURVIVE THROUGH THE AGES!

Stalking silently through gardens on the outskirts of town, Rumpy's nose alerts him to some danger. A pair of eyes are watching him from the shadows.

SURVIVAL SKILL 5 SOMETIMES, DANGER CAN BE SMELT EVEN IF IT CAN'T BE SEEN. RUMPY QUICKLY SLIPS AWAY, AVOIDING AN ATTACK.

POOH, A STINKY FOX!

HMM, WONDER WHAT CATS TASTE LIKE.

Suddenly, a fierce dog leaps out of the dark. In half a second Rumpy is up a tree and out of danger.

FOXES, DOGS, HUH, THEY CAN'T CATCH ME!

SURVIVAL SKILL 6
WITH HIS SHARP CLAWS AND POWERFUL LEG MUSCLES RUMPY HAS ESCAPED DANGER ONCE MORE!

The dog has moved on and Rumpy continues his journey. He finds a pool of water to quench his thirst. Rumpy quickly detects that the water is not safe to drink.

SURVIVAL SKILL 7
CATS HAVE A TASTE-SMELL SENSE THAT WARNS THEM IF SOMETHING IS ROTTEN OR POISONOUS.

YUK, NO WAY!

SNIFF!

The main road is quieter at night and having crossed it safely, Rumpy visits McUdder's Farm.

He decides to catch himself some supper.

HELLO, DINNER!

The sun is rising as Rumpy strolls into the garden of Orchard Cottage. He hears the rustling of a bird in the apple tree and decides to catch a meal for his friend, Daisy.

He pounces on the startled sparrow but loses his footing on the narrow branch.

SURVIVAL SKILL 9
It's a three-metre drop to the ground but Rumpy turns in the air and lands safely on his feet.

Spotting his best friend by the house, Rumpy trots up and drops his tasty offering at her feet.

Zak was impressed. "Woah! That's as good as anything you've done, maybe better!" he said.

Dad agreed. "Well, yes, it is an excellent piece of work. Maybe you could put it on our website."

OK, so it was good. But I didn't want other people's drawings on my site!

"Daisy didn't send it to go on our website!" I snapped. Then, calming down, I explained. "She says it's just a school project but there's more to it than that. I think she hopes it might persuade Lizzy to untape Rumpy's cat flap and let him go back to Orchard Cottage."

Dad seemed to understand. "Hmm. But you know, there's no way Lizzy's going to let Rumpy out. He's back home now and he'll be with his proper owner in a few days. I'm not sure what'll happen when Camilla sees him. But that's got nothing to do with us or Daisy Braithwaite."

Later that day we heard from Lizzy Rake.

From: Lizzy Rake

Hi Doug and Beth

Thank you so much for your emails. Your idea for the collar message, dieting advice and suggestions for keeping Rumpy amused are most welcome.

I'm sure you must have been as surprised as Daisy and I were to hear about all the people who had been feeding Rumpy. And you may still be wondering who bought the red collar. Well now we know! It was Fergus Finnigan the local fishmonger. He's been feeding fish scraps to Tubby Tom (as he calls Rumpy) for weeks. He hadn't emailed me because he doesn't have a computer, but he called round yesterday after reading the Daily Pyddle. Rumpy was front-page news!

THE DAILY PYDDLE

RUMPY RUMPUSS!

~

FAT CAT FLEECES LOCALS.

Rumpy, the cat with no tail, has been charming his way into Pyddlehampton homes on a never-ending quest for food. Life, in recent weeks, has been one big lunch for the fat cat. But the frequent feasts have made Rumpy dumpy.

"The banquet is over!" says Lizzy Rake, who has been looking after Rumpy while her sister is away. "Camilla will be back very soon," she explained, "and I must get her precious cat slim before she arrives. Camilla intends to enter Rumpy in the Furrington Cat Show in January. I don't think the judges would be too impressed with his present shape!"

AN ANXIOUS LIZZY RAKE

Miss Rake continued, "I'd like to thank everybody for agreeing to stop Rumpy's extra meals. He's a loveable rogue and has made many new friends.

"Pyddlehampton Animal Shelter has many other cats that are looking for loving homes. Perhaps Rumpy's new friends might consider rescuing a cat of their own. I do hope so!"

So if you're one of Rumpy's old friends and miss the fat fella's company, why not consider Lizzy's suggestion?

PYDDLEHAMPTON ANIMAL SHELTER P.A.S

Looking for a friendly, cuddly, amusing, interesting, independent, easy-to-keep pet? For only a small charge you can...

RESCUE A CAT!

Here at Pyddlehampton Animal Shelter we have over 20 cats and kittens looking for loving homes.

All cats are vaccinated, neutered, wormed, de-flea'd, microchipped and ready to go!
Telephone Jan on
Pyddlehampton 667859

SO PAY US A VISIT AND SHAKE PAWS WITH A NEW PAL!

Who'd have thought that one cat could cause so much interest?

Rumpy's not very happy with his prison sentence! But even though I know about Fergus, I've decided to keep the cat indoors until Camilla gets back. I know Daisy isn't happy about it but I can't risk him crossing that road again.

Poor Daisy. I don't think she'd ever cared for an animal until she met Rumpy. I know how fond she is of my sister's cat – she's made that very clear in her cartoon strip. Have you seen it? I must admit it's very good – BUT I'M NOT LETTING HIM OUT!

If it was my decision, I'd happily let Rumpy live up at Orchard Cottage where he wants to be. But his real owner will be home in a couple of weeks, and I'm not looking forward to her returning!

ONLY TWO WEEKS 'TIL SHE GETS BACK!

Best wishes
Lizzy

Dad was smiling. "Just as I predicted. That cat's going nowhere!"

"Yes, all right, Dad," I said. "No need to sound quite so pleased."

Another school week passed (quite quickly, actually). Three days until the Christmas hols and only six until Camilla got back.

The next time I heard from Daisy she was more cheerful than I thought she'd be.

From: Daisy

Hi Beth

Hope you're well.

Rumpy hasn't been released from prison so I go to see him during visiting hours (Saturday mornings while Lizzy's working) and help him work out!

He has ten minutes with the fishing-rod toy and ten minutes running up and down the stairs after me! When he's bored with that I give him a good brush and his mid-morning snack (don't panic, it's all part of his strict diet). Anyway, after we've done all that, Rumpy sits on my lap and we watch a video until Lizzy gets back.

I think he likes that bit best. Sometimes he purrs so loudly that I have to turn up the volume on the telly!

Rumpy has lost some weight but Lizzy says Camilla is sure to be unhappy when she sees him.

I'm trying to make the most of him until she returns. Bet I don't see much of him when she does.

Love from
Daisy

"Time's running out," Dad said when he saw the message. "Lizzy should have started the slimming programme sooner. I reckon there's going to be trouble!"

The week passed and Camilla returned home. We'd soon find out if Dad's predictions were correct...

Cream Puff

"Thanks, ever so!" said Mrs Parker-Carwell, scribbling her signature on the cheque and handing it to Dad. "Baldy's been very sore! I do so hope this cream works."

"It should help," Dad said, opening the door for her. "And keep Baldy out of the conservatory on sunny days!"

Mrs Parker-Carwell tottered to her shiny Rolls and put Baldy's carrying cage on the back seat. Only when she'd driven off (back to Carwell Mansion) did I dare speak.

"That is the weirdest pet I've ever seen!" I gasped. "A bald cat? I mean, it's so creepy!"

Dad smiled. "I quite agree," he said, "Baldy's a Peterbald cat, they're quite rare. Not my cup of tea but Mrs P-C obviously loves her!"

"And she had sunburn?"

"That's right. Even the winter sun, shining through the glass in her conservatory, is enough to scorch Baldy's hairless little body. I guess if we walked around naked in the sun all day, we'd have problems, too."

Zak walked in. "Yeah, you'd get locked up, for starters."

"Yes, ha ha," I said. "We're talking about treatment for bald cats, in case you didn't realize."

"Buy them a fur coat!" he suggested. "Remember that American advert we did a few weeks ago?"

Zak was right (annoyingly). Fur coats for cats really do exist!

INTERNET VET ADVERTISEMENTS

PURCHASE PET PRODUCTS FROM AROUND THE WORLD!

 IS YOUR CAT HAIRLESS, WRINKLED, COLD, BALD AND SHIVERING?

GET HER ONE OF OUR

FURRYCOTES

AND SHE'LL LOVE YOU FOREVER

Made from synthetic fur, these coats will keep your hairless cat as warm as toast. And if she's worried about becoming toast with no hair to protect her from the sun, a FURRYCOTE will solve this problem too!

CHAMPION PETERBALD, "COOT" MODELS OUR BEST-SELLING "COW" DESIGN

OTHER FURRYCOTE DESIGNS INCLUDE: DALMATION ZEBRA CHEETAH

"I can't imagine Archie strutting round the house looking like a cow!" Dad laughed.

Zak agreed. "There's no need. He's a proper cat, not like Mrs P-C's mog – a baldy weirdo!"

It just slipped out. "Like Dad, you mean?"

"Yes, thank you, Betts," he said. "I haven't lost all my hair. Anyway, haven't you two got homework to do?"

Rats. I should have kept my mouth shut. But then we were saved by an email from Daisy.

From: Daisy

HELP!

Hi Beth

Camilla's back! And guess what she said when she saw Rumpy...

Not much, actually! She did make a few rude remarks about Lizzy's incompetence but the truth is she's more interested in her new pet. Yes, Camilla brought a new cat back with her. He's called Cream Puff and she's totally obsessed with him!

All she talks about now is how well Cream Puff will do in the Furrington Cat Show. She combs him, trims his fur, ties ribbons in his hair and feeds him little pieces of salmon! She seems to have totally forgotten about her beautiful Manx cat.

I don't suppose Rumpy's bothered about not going to the Cat Show. But he is bothered about being kept indoors most of the time, and he's been put on an even stricter diet!

I'm keeping in touch with Lizzy. She suggested that I ask my parents for a kitten, maybe even a Manx. I expect the twins would like that. The last time Rumpy visited, they said, "Nice fat cat!" and not "Naughty fat cat!"

I'll think about it, anyway.

Thanks to you, Zak and your dad for the help you've given.

Hope you all have a good Christmas.

Love
Daisy

PS Did you like my cartoon strip?

Whoops, I'd forgotten to thank her for that. I replied later with a short Happy Christmas email. I asked her to send me an update on things in the New Year. I didn't have to wait that long.

Two days before Christmas, I was tidying the office with Dad when a message came through. The Rumpy story wasn't quite over, it seemed...

From: Daisy

HELP!

Hi Beth

Just had to write and tell you – Rumpy's been up to his tricks again!

It all happened yesterday. Lizzy phoned me on her mobile. She said something big was happening down in Pyddlehampton Market Square. She couldn't stop to chat but she told me to get down there quick! I arrived on Mum's bike, 20 minutes later, to find a group of people looking up at a large Christmas tree. The police had stopped the traffic while a fire engine positioned itself close to the tree. I made my way over to where Lizzy and Fergus Finnigan were comforting a sobbing Camilla.

"Oh my poor Cream Puff!" she wailed. Then her expression changed from despair to anger. "And that bad, bad cat, Rumpy. He's completely changed since I went away. AND IT'S ALL YOUR FAULT, ELIZABETH!"

Lizzy didn't answer back. Instead she looked over to me and silently pointed to the top of the tree. Now I understood.

Cream Puff, meowing piteously, was balanced on a thin branch with Rumpy hissing and swiping at him from below.

"First he chases my darling Cream Puff to the top of that wretched tree and now he's trying to knock him off!" Camilla wailed.

This was too much for Lizzy. "Well, what do you expect? Rumpy's been locked in the

kitchen for over a month with Cream Puff making faces at him through the cat-flap door!" Fergus was nodding in agreement.

Looking around, I saw many of Rumpy's old friends, their worried faces peering up at the tree. Pierre Pallette was clutching an Indian take-away. WPC Dixon was controlling the traffic. Freda and Mike McUdder were watching events from the cab of their muddy Landrover. Father McHat had just taken a carol service. He was standing in the church doorway with Matt Pawsworth and his mum. And Terry Ball was standing by the fire engine jotting down notes. A fireman stood at the top of the ladder that had, by now, almost reached the cats.

A terrified Cream Puff wailed louder than ever as the fireman reached out with a big net. At almost the same time, Rumpy took a final swipe at Camilla's precious cat and knocked him off the branch...

There was a gasp from the crowd, followed by a sigh of relief as Cream Puff fell into the net. The fireman decided to bring Cream Puff down before trying to rescue Rumpy.

I ran towards the fire engine with Camilla close behind. "Be careful with that cat!" she shouted. "I'm entering him in a competition in three weeks!" She reached up and took the trembling Cream Puff from the fireman's hands. Camilla didn't seem bothered that Rumpy was still in danger.

I raised my hand in the crowd to catch the fireman's attention. "Please hurry!" I shouted. "Rumpy looks as if he's about to jump!"

And that's exactly what the tubby cat did. He jumped on to the top rung of the ladder and walked down all by himself. What a hero! And when he reached the bottom of the ladder we all cheered and clapped. It was brilliant.

The fireman passed the purring cat down to me. "There you are, miss. All safe and sound!" he said.

I hugged Rumpy and kissed him on the head. "He doesn't actually belong to me," I answered.

"Oh, I think he does," came a voice from behind. Looking round I saw a smiling Lizzy. "Camilla says she never wants to see Rumpy again!" Then she leaned forward and tickled Rumpy under the chin. "Take him back to Orchard Cottage where he belongs," she said.

And that's what I did. Can you imagine a better Christmas present? Rumpy belongs to me!

Love from
Daisy x

PS I think maybe I'm going to enjoy living in the countryside, after all!

A good ending, eh? Although actually it wasn't quite the end. In the New Year this newspaper cutting came from Lizzy Rake.

~DAILY PYDDLE~

Minutes from the first meeting of the PYDDLEHAMPTON URBAN RESCUE & REHOMING SOCIETY ~ a new charity for homeless cats

ABSENCE APOLOGIES
From Father Sean McHat who was away in Lourdes with the Pyddle Abbey Sisters of Mercy. Mother McCready is reported to be looking after Pew, Father Sean's new cat. Also from Fergus Finnigan who'd taken Lizzy Rake to the cinema (again).

CHAIRMAN'S REPORT
Newly elected chairman, Terry Ball, wished everybody a happy New Year and welcomed them to this first meeting. He was pleased to announce that his three-legged cat, Tripod, was settling in well and hoped that all other rescued cats were enjoying life in their new homes.

TREASURER'S REPORT

Treasurer, Pamela Pawsworth, announced the winner of the "Guess the weight of Rumpy" competition (Mrs K Goodbody) and confirmed that all money raised (£6.47pence) would go to Jan at the Animal Shelter.

SECRETARY'S REPORT

Secretary, Freda McUdder, announced that tickets for the Furrington Cat Show were still available at £3.50. This price includes the entrance fee, and a token for a cup of tea and a slice of cake in the refreshment tent.

ANY OTHER BUSINESS

The chairman introduced our Guest of Honour, Miss Daisy Braithwaite. Daisy had drawn a splendid logo for our newly formed society. The circular design featured none other than the famous tailless cat, Rumpy. It was proposed by WPC Dixon that without this loveable character, the society would never have been formed. The proposal was seconded with a warm round of applause.

P.U.R.R.S

THE INTERNET VET

WIN PRIZES

WHY NOT VISIT OUR WEBSITE?

We're at:

WWW.INTERNET-VET.CO.UK

PET STUFF — Stacks of fascinating facts and other PET STUFF

WIN STUFF — Take part in our competitions and WIN STUFF!

BOOK STUFF — BOOK STUFF – the latest info on forthcoming titles

LINK STUFF — Check out other pet sites on the LINK STUFF page

THE INTERNET VET

Also in this series:

Help!
My dog can't stop farting

Help!
Something's eaten my hamster